3/00

D0537073

Look What Came From

Russia

by
Miles Harvey

Franklin Watts

A Division of Grolier Publishing

New York London Hong Kong Sydney

Danbury, Connecticut

Series Concept: Shari Joffe
Design: Steve Marton

Library of Congress Cataloging-in-Publication Data

Harvey, Miles.
    Look What Came From Russia / by Miles Harvey.
        p. cm. — (Look what came from)
    Includes bibliographical references and index.
    Summary: Describes many things that originally came
from Russia, including inventions, sports and games, food,
fashion, musical instruments, animals, arts and crafts,
and words.
    ISBN 0-531-11499-6 (lib. bdg.)   0-531-15966-3 (pbk.)
    1. Russia—Civilization—Juvenile literature.
2. Civilization—Russian influences—Juvenile literature.
[1. Russia—Civilization.   2. Civilization—Russian
influences.] I. Title.   II. Series.
DK32.H38   1999
947—dc21   98-35948
                                                   CIP
                                                   AC

Visit Franklin Watts on the Internet at:
http://publishing.grolier.com

Photo credits © : Animals Animals: front cover top right (Robert Pearcy),
20 (M. Colbeck/OSF); Charise Mericle: 5; Christie's Images: front cover top left,
1, border on pages 4 and 6-32, 22 left, middle; Corbis-Bettmann: 17 left
(Agence France Presse); Envision: 7 left (Agence Top), 7 right, 9 top left,
23 bottom right, 27 (Vladimir Morozov), 9 top right (Steven Needham), 9 bottom
(Paul Poplis), 32 left (Osentoski & Zoda); MIR Agency: 8, 10, 15 right;
Nancie Battaglia: 16; NHPA: 21 right (Melvin Grey); Panos Pictures: 15 left
(Jon Spaull); Photo Researchers: 12, 13 left, top right (Novosti/Science Photo
Library), 18 (Axel/Jacana), 19 left (Jeanne White), 21 left (Kenneth W. Fink),
25 bottom left (Elisabeth Weiland); Sovfoto/Eastfoto: front cover bottom, 4
bottom left, top right, 13 bottom right, 22 right-23 left (Tass), 6 left, 11, 23 top
right, 24 right (Novosti), 4 bottom right, 6 left, 13 middle right, 19 right;
Superstock, Inc.: stamp on back cover (Ernest Manewal), 3, 17 middle, 25 top
(Hermitage Museum, St. Petersburg, Russia/Leonid Bogdanov), front cover
background, 6 right, 14; Tony Stone Images, Inc.: 24 left (Cliff Hollenbeck),
25 right (Art Wolfe)

Contents

Greetings from Russia! 4

Food 6

Inventions 10

Space Travel 12

Fashion 14

Sports and Games 16

Animals 18

Arts and Crafts 22

Musical Instruments 24

Words 25

A Recipe from Russia 26

How Do You Say . . . ? 28

To Find Out More 29

Glossary 30

Index 31

Greetings from Russia!

Russia is a huge place. For many years, it was part of a gigantic land called the Soviet Union. In 1989, the Soviet Union split up into several smaller countries. But even so, Russia is still the biggest country in the world. It is so large, in fact, that it has almost twice as much land as the United States!

To get to Russia, you would have to take a very long plane trip. But you can learn a lot about this incredible land without leaving your home. That's because many things in the world around you had their start in Russia. So, come on! Let's find out about all the cool stuff that comes from Russia!

The flag of Russia

Russian paper money and coins

4

Food

Caviar

Modern-day Russian wine

No one knows who invented **wine.**
But some experts think this drink came
from an area near present-day Russia.
People in the Caucasus mountain region
have been making wine for as long as
7,000 years.

Today, people in Russia still love good
food and drink. Do you know what **caviar** is?

6

Caviar on blini

Blintzes

It's a food made of salted fish eggs. Russians adore this gooey treat. The best and hardest-to-find kind of caviar in the world comes from Russia. It is known as golden caviar, and it comes from a fish called the sterlet.

Sometimes caviar is eaten with *blini*, a Russian kind of pancake. You may know these pancakes as **blintzes.**

more food

Although mushrooms grow in many parts of the world, in Russia, **picking wild mushrooms** has been a special tradition for hundreds of years. In the late summer and early fall, thousands of people from big cities go out to the country to search for these delicious treats. But they have to be very careful. Some kinds of mushrooms are poisonous.

Russians like to begin many of their meals with snacks known as **zakuski.** These snacks might include everything from hard-cooked eggs to cold fish. After the zakuski comes

Russian man picking wild mushrooms

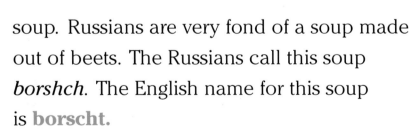

Zakuski

Borscht

soup. Russians are very fond of a soup made out of beets. The Russians call this soup *borshch*. The English name for this soup is **borscht.**

When the soup is finished, it's time for the main part of the meal. One famous main course served in Russia is called **chicken Kiev.**

Chicken Kiev

Inventions

More than 7,000 years ago, people in Russia began speaking to each other in the **Indo-European language.** This ancient language soon began to spread to other areas. Over the centuries, it turned into many new languages, including Russian, Spanish, Greek, German, and English.

Early example of Russian writing

Irrigation

But that's not the only famous Russian invention. Some experts think people in Russia came up with the idea for **irrigation** about 6,000 years ago. Irrigation is a way to bring water to plants in areas where there is not enough rain. People dig ditches that lead from rivers and lakes into farm fields. The ditches fill up with water. This water helps the plants in the fields grow tall!

Another invention that comes from Russia is the **nuclear power plant.** Nuclear power plants supply electricity for millions of people around the world. The first one began operation in Russia in 1954. Today, a number of countries, including the United States, use nuclear power plants. Many people, however, worry that they are unsafe. In 1986, there was a bad accident at a Soviet nuclear

The first nuclear power plant

power plant near a Ukrainian town called Chernobyl. The accident killed some people and made many others very sick. Since then, people have worked harder to make sure that nuclear power plants are safe.

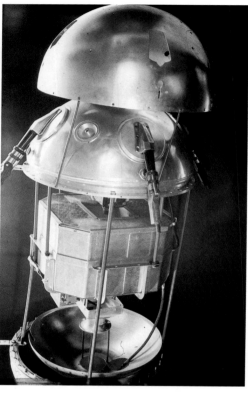

Space Travel

A **satellite** is a very special machine that is sent up into space. Once it is there, it begins to circle around the Earth. Because it is so high up, a satellite can broadcast television and telephone signals from one part of the world to another. It can also do many other things, such as help scientists predict the weather. People from Russia launched the first satellite into outer space in 1957.

The Russians also made other important contributions to space travel. For instance, in 1961, they launched the first **manned spaceship.** A manned spaceship is a rocket ship that is flown by a human being. Russian space explorers are called *cosmonauts*. The **first person to go into outer space** was a cosmonaut named Yuri Gagarin. In 1963, a cosmonaut named Valentina Tereshkova became the **first woman in space.**

Launch of the first manned space flight

Yuri Gagarin

Valentina
Tereshkova

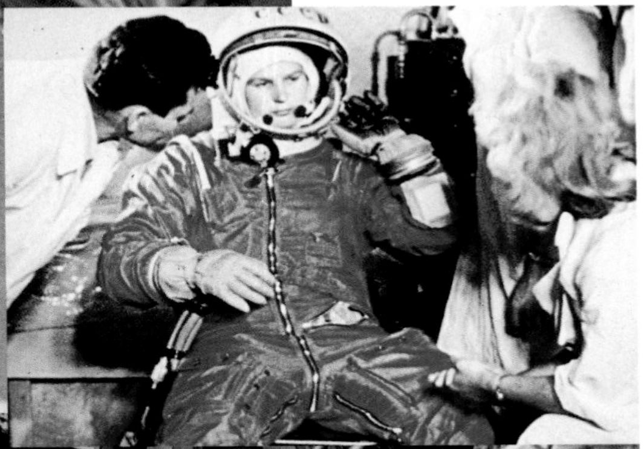

In 1971, people in Russia launched the first **space station.** A space station is kind of like a house floating in outer space. People go there to live for months at a time. While in the space station, they do scientific experiments.

Cosmonauts inside a Russian space station

Man wearing a shapka

Fashion

Russia gets extremely cold in the winter, so people have to wear very warm clothes. One famous kind of hat that comes from Russia is the **shapka.** It is made of wool or fur to guard against chilly weather. One well-known type of fur that comes from Russia is called **astrakhan.** It comes from a kind of lamb.

Man wearing a shapka made of astrakhan

Woman selling valenki boots

Another traditional kind of Russian clothing is the **valenki** boot. These boots are made of felt. They offer great protection against the cold.

Sports and Games

Today, skiing is a sport. But for many years, it was an important type of transportation. The oldest **skis** in the world were found in Russia. They are at least 8,000 years old!

modern-day skis

No one knows exactly who invented the game of **chess.** But some experts think it came from Russia about 1,800 years ago. Millions of people in Russia still love this incredible game. In fact, many of the greatest chess players in the world have come from Russia, including Gary Kasparov and Anatoly Karpov.

Some Russian games are much newer than chess. One of them is a famous computer game called **Tetris.** It was invented by a Russian scientist named Alexey Pajitnov.

Tetris

Chess champion Gary Kasparov

Old Russian chess pieces

Animals

Is your pet Russian? Maybe so. Some popular breeds of cats originally came from Russia, including the **Russian blue.** A few kinds of dogs also originally came from Russia. One of them is the **borzoi,** which was originally used to protect human beings from wolves.

Russian blue

Borzoi

People in Russia love to ride horses. One of the most popular kinds of Russian horses is the **don.** This was a favorite horse of the cossacks, a famous group of Russian warriors.

Don

19

more animals

Baikal seals

Another important Russian animal is the **Baikal seal,** the smallest kind of seal in the world. It can be found only in Lake Baikal, which is located in an area of Russia known as Siberia. Lake Baikal is the world's deepest lake. Unfortunately, it is very polluted.

20

Baikal teal

One kind of bird that lives near the lake is the **Baikal teal.** Every now and then one of these birds loses its way and shows up in the United States!

Another Russian bird is the **Siberian jay.** It lives in the Siberian taiga, the largest forest in the world.

Siberian jay

Because humans have poured lots of dangerous chemicals in the water, many Baikal seals have died.

Arts and Crafts

Fabergé egg

In 1884, the Russian emperor wanted to give his wife a present for Easter. He asked a jewelry maker named Carl Fabergé to create a special gift. It was an Easter egg—but a very unusual one. That's because it was made out of gold and jewels! In the years that followed, he made many more of these **Fabergé eggs.** Today, other artists make similar ones. People all over the world collect these treasures.

Nesting dolls are another cool kind of Russian art. They look like regular dolls. But guess what? When you pull one of them apart, a smaller doll is inside. And inside that is an even smaller doll!

People in the Russian village of Palekh are famous around the world for making **painted boxes.**

Fabergé egg

They make these beautiful boxes out of papier mâché. Then they paint lovely pictures on them. Finally, they put a clear kind of paint known as lacquer over the top. Some of the paintbrushes they use are made from the hair of squirrel tails.

The Russian towns of Khokhloma and Semyonov make another amazing type of art. It is known as **golden Khokhloma.** Artists from these towns carve wood into

Top of a Russian lacquered box

vases, candlesticks, and other items for the dinner table. Then they paint them with bright colors, including red, green, and gold.

Nesting dolls

Golden Khokhloma items

Musical Instruments

People in Russia use many of the same musical instruments that are used in North America and Europe. But they also have some instruments of their own. The **balalaika** is considered the national instrument of Russia. It looks a little bit like a guitar, but has a triangular body and only three strings. The balalaika comes in several different sizes.

Another old-fashioned Russian instrument is the **gusli.** It has up to 36 strings. People play this instrument by plucking the strings with both hands.

Large balalaika

Gusli

Words

We get some of our words from Russia. One Russian word we use is **"troika."** In Russia, this word refers to a type of sleigh or wagon pulled by three horses. But in English, it is used to describe all sorts of things that come in groups of three.

"Czar" is the Russian word for "emperor." In English, however, this word is used as an informal way to describe many different kinds of leaders.

One more word that comes from Russia is **"babushka."** It is a kind of scarf that some women wear on their heads. In Russia, however, the word also has another meaning. There, a babushka is a grandmother!

Troika

A Recipe from Russia

For hundreds of years, people in Russia have been eating a delicious dessert called **kissel.** You can make raspberry kissel yourself, with the help of an adult.

To start, you'll need the following ingredients:
- 2 cups of fresh raspberries
- 5 cups of water
- 3 tablespoons of sugar
- 1/4 cup of potato starch

You'll also need the following equipment:
- a medium-sized saucepan
- a measuring cup
- a fine-mesh strainer
- a big spoon
- a large bowl
- a small bowl
- a whisk
- serving glasses
- spoons

You can do the first part of the recipe by yourself.
1. Wash your hands.
2. Wash the raspberries.
3. Put the raspberries into the saucepan.
4. Put 4 cups of water into the saucepan.

You'll need an adult to do the next part of the recipe, but you can help out by reading the instructions out loud.
1. Put the saucepan on top of the stove. Adjust the heat to medium and bring the water to a boil.
2. Reduce the heat to medium-low and cook until the raspberries get mushy—about 10 or 15 minutes.
3. Turn off the heat and allow the saucepan to cool until the water is safe for kids to touch.

Now you can work on the recipe by yourself again, with an adult watching.

1. Set the strainer on top of a large bowl.
2. Carefully pour the water from the saucepan through the strainer into the bowl. The cooked raspberries will now be sitting in the strainer.
3. With the big spoon, mash the raspberries so that the soft parts fall down into the bowl.
4. Pour the water and mashed berries back into the saucepan.
5. Add the 3 tablespoons of sugar to the saucepan. Set the saucepan aside.
6. In a small bowl, mix the potato starch with 1 cup of water, stirring carefully to make sure there are no lumps.

You'll need an adult to do the next part of the recipe.

1. Bring the contents of the saucepan to a boil, stirring over medium heat.
2. Reduce the heat to low and simmer the mixture until the sugar is completely dissolved. That should take about 2 or 3 minutes.
3. Whisk the potato-starch mixture into the simmering berry mixture.

Kissel

4. Bring the whole thing to a boil, stirring hard until the mixture gets thick.
5. Remove the saucepan from the heat and cool until the mixture is safe for kids to touch. Stir the mixture from time to time while it's cooling.

You can do the final part of the recipe by yourself, with an adult watching.

1. Carefully spoon the mixture into the serving glasses.
2. Put the glasses in the refrigerator until the mixture is cold.
3. Grab a spoon! You're ready to taste kissel!

How do you say....?

People in Russia use a different alphabet than we do. It is called the Cyrillic alphabet. But look at the words below—some letters from the Cyrillic alphabet and our alphabet are the same!

English	Russian	How to pronounce it
good morning	Доброе утро	DAW-bruh-yeh OO-truh
goodbye	До свидания	duh svee-DAH-nee-yuh
please	Пожалуйста	pah-ZHAL-stuh
thank you	Спасибо	spah-SEE-buh
boots	сапог	sah-PAWK
chicken	курица	KOO-reet-suh
egg	яйцо	yee-TSAW
mushrooms	грибы	gree-BEE

To find out more

Here are some other resources to help you learn more about Russia:

Books

Flint, David C. **The Russian Federation.** Millbrook Press, 1992.

Haskins, Jim. **Count Your Way Through Russia.** Carolrhoda Books, 1988.

Lye, Keith. **Passport to Russia.** Franklin Watts, 1996.

Russia: Then and Now. Lerner Publications, 1992.

Whyte, Harlinah. **Festivals of the World: Russia.** Gareth Stevens, 1997.

Organizations and Online Sites

Embassy of the Russian Federation
Information Office
1706 18th Street, NW
Washington, DC 20009
http://www.russianembassy. org/embassy.html

Map of Russia
http://www.lib.utexas.edu/ Libs/PCL/Map_collection/ commonwealth/Russia.94.jpg
Check out this online map of Russia, provided by the University of Texas at Austin.

Russia—CityNet
http://www.city.net/countries/ russia/
Find out today's weather in Russia—and discover a great list of web links about the country.

Russian National Tourist Office
800 Third Avenue, Suite 3101
New York, NY 10022
http://www.russiatravel.com/

Glossary

ancient very, very old

astrakhan fur, used in clothing and hats, that comes from a certain type of curly-coated lamb found in Russia

beet a dark-red root vegetable

broadcast to send by radio or television

gigantic very, very large

irrigation a way of bringing water from lakes or rivers to fields

launched sent off

poisonous something that is harmful or deadly to a living thing if eaten or touched

polluted dirty

predict to know or tell that something is going to happen

satellite an object or vehicle sent up into space to circle the Earth or the moon

space station a large satellite designed to be lived in for long periods of time and to be used as a base for space experiments

taiga a forest that has a moist, cold climate and is made up mostly of pine trees

traditional handed down from generation to generation

Index

animals, 18-21

arts and crafts, 22-23

astrakhan, 14

babushka, 25

Baikal seal, 20

Baikal teal, 21

balalaika, 24

blini, 7

blintzes, 7

borscht, 9

borzoi, 18

caviar, 6

chess, 17

chicken Kiev, 9

czar, 25

don, 19

Fabergé eggs, 22

fashion, 14-15

food, 6-9

Gagarin, Yuri, 12

golden Khokhloma, 23

gusli, 24

Indo-European language, 10

inventions, 10-11

irrigation, 11

kissel, 26

manned spaceship, 12

musical instruments, 24

nesting dolls, 22

nuclear power plant, 11

painted boxes, 22

Russian blue, 18

satellite, 12

shapka, 14

Siberian jay, 21

skis, 16

Soviet Union, 4

space station, 13

space travel, 12-13

sports and games, 16-17

Tereshkova, Valentina, 12

Tetris, 17

troika, 25

valenki boot, 15

wild mushrooms, 8

wine, 6

words, 25

zakuski, 8

Look what doesn't come from Russia!

Have you ever tried **Russian dressing** on a salad? It's delicious, but it doesn't come from Russia. It was invented in the United States!

Meet the Author

Miles Harvey has written several books for young people. He lives in Chicago. This book is dedicated to his nieces and nephews: Gabe, Justin, Camille, August, Sam, Harry, Will, and Maggie.